Sing What You See

Sing What You See

Poems by

Holli Terrell-Cavalluzzi

© 2025 Holli Terrell-Cavalluzzi. All rights reserved.
This material may not be reproduced in any form, published,
reprinted, recorded, performed, broadcast,
rewritten, or redistributed without
the explicit permission of Holli Terrell-Cavalluzzi.
All such actions are strictly prohibited by law.

Cover design by Shay Culligan
Cover photo by arlindphotography on Pexels
Author photo by Holli Terrell-Cavalluzzi

ISBN: 978-1-63980-682-9
Library of Congress Control Number: 2025934251

Kelsay Books
502 South 1040 East, A-119
American Fork, Utah 84003
Kelsaybooks.com

Acknowledgments

Thank you to the following publications, in which versions of these poems previously appeared:

Flora Fiction: "Togetherness," "The Call of the Wild," "Cherry Blossoms"
New Note Poetry: "A Prayer"

Contents

Dear Oaks	11
A Man Stands	12
Hourglass	14
This Midnight	15
Someone Must	16
From the Left	17
The Red Couch	19
Leaves are Falling	21
Classic	22
Spell	24
After Reading a Bazooka Bubble Gum Wrapper	25
Body Politic	26
A Call of the Wild	27
Country Road	28
Now and Again	29
Between this Year and Next	30
To Make Sacred	31
Cicada	33
Summer Prayer	34
The Snail	36
Movement on Squares in Dupont Circle	37
Crossing the Lines	38
New Clothes, Old Letters	39
Threshold	40
Ferris Wheel	41
Us	42
Freedom Meditation	43
A Prayer	44
Cherry Blossoms	45

Dear Oaks

Occupants of Georgia Park,
whose catalogue-ordered retro fountain,
breathtaking as any devoted antecedent,
so enchants a woman that she doesn't wait
to find the gate, but lobs her plastic bottle
and follows after, climbing up
and clambering her robust hips over,
and wades in the pool.

Dear Oaks' old residents,
your seven-pointed leaves,
jutting, enchanting,
green me with stories
in ghostly cloaks of moss.

Dear Oaks, it's you who lure me,
lulled to a meditative state
on your shaded bench,
in no ordinary silence of shining leaves,
while the woman palms her bottle.

Dear Oaks, I won't stay to see
if she finds what she seeks
under the waterfall.

A Man Stands

—after Langston Hughes

at the intersection.

Shirtless, collarbones
visible under his elastic skin.
On his cardboard sign,
a handwritten note recalls
the label *Fragile, Handle with Care*
I wrote on a box for shipping,
but his *Will work for money,
have a blessed day,*
gives me what I need:
candor in what's muddled.

I wonder what happened
to his dream. Postponed?
Lost in onrushing traffic?

The dream must once
have been honeyed,
before the streets
claimed him, before
he claimed this corner.

Worn cardboard
calling for response,
*a heavier load
than I can guess,
set to quietly explode?*

I reach past
the veteran's message,
responding
with a meal
and dollars
from my car window
for his service,
like a drive-thru,

his un-wondering eyes
on my wondering ones,
My shaking hand grasped
briefly by his steady one.

Hourglass

Mostly, sand sweeps,
swirls and falls
through the opening,
but sometimes,
a few grains
stick together
as if they sought
to stop time
for a while,
to remind me
that time is in my mind.

I heard a writer
unravel an hourglass
as a portal with no
conceivable entrance.

I watch the indifferent
sand leading
toward definite ends
and infinite beginnings.

It could care less
if it's flipped or not.
I give it meaning,
as I must to everything.

As the two halves,
thin as wasp waist,
I can't imagine not breaking.

This Midnight

The particulars
this midnight:
satin sheets, cotton pillow,
dim light parting the windowsill,
like day parts night.
Saffron curtain tassels
undulate like waving hands
as the silver ceiling fan
brushes the air,
as does my breath.
A chill raises goosebumps,
the body possessed
by solace; flesh holds
muscle and bone
like no one's business.

Someone Must

Someone must
have accidentally
let the water bug in,
since it's too big
to slip through a crevice.

It runs
to crumbs
and sifted flour meant
for oatmeal pancakes,
drifted on the floor.

When someone asks me
to kill the armored,
crab-antlered creature,
I lift and ferry it
with a newspaper outside,

in hopes others—and I,
are granted leniency,
to run with the wild,
once in a while.

From the Left

Scotland's cars
steer and drive
on the other side
of what I've known.

Nearly every turn
merges onto highways
and in or out
of roundabouts,
to the left
of what I expect.
Your left side,
your quiet profile driving
new to me, highlights
how blaring I can be.
Climbing the highlands,
we pull onto left shoulders
for pictures of endless
lavender-hued heather.

When rain soaks
the road's shoulders into mud,
we head left down the mountain.

Down the mountain streams
to rivers, to sea, down
the building sides and streets,
down drains to sea.

A quaint town,
where time stretches
lochs thin as rivers.
River Ness has
a mythical creature,
a serpentine creature
seen only by believers
just often enough
to keep the legend going.
Surprise keeps finding me
from the left,
on a verso page
in Leakey's Bookshop.
Words disperse
as birds, gestures, people,
fog suggesting
the serpentine
as it wends,

unbridling me
to imagine anything
is possible in a left-winding life.

The Red Couch

It stared bereft
from the road I travel,
only half-noticing the world
outside my head.

I imagine
an abandoned wife,
banishing memories
of plush velvet seductions,
dumping the loveseat.

A red motel for rodents,
safe haven between cushions
and springs from stalking foxes.

Maybe a seamstress
will haul it off in a rusty truck bed,
strip its faded elegance
and redress it in paisley
to woo a collector—

my uncle, who'll invite me
over for tea, where I'll sit
absorbing its creativity
as he enthuses over
how it matches the dragon lamp
he brought back from Japan.

But such romances
vanish with the couch.
I'll miss my totem
so much that I secretly
want to leave flowers.

Leaves Are Falling

Bella in the rose leaves
dripping from the bush,
after their long season
photosynthesizing
to grow pink roses.
Blue Great Dane pulls me
with her leash as I try to match
her long stride.
Bella for the memory
of my gondola ride in Italy.

Bella, gone to dawn shadows,
opening wings over autumn's
shorter days, partially illuminating
the yard where we played.

Bella in the rose bush,
denuded of all but thorns,
protecting itself deciduously
from winter's cold,
bereft this year
of her giant paw prints.

Bella in spring's greens,
rose canes reaching
from decomposition
to bloom new roses
as I walk my other dog,
who is no longer jealous
of my attention.

Classic

A crow circling overhead
walks me into new crosswalk paint,
yellowing my shoes.
Rue ribbons my mind
as I rubberneck
its black-cloaked path.

Crows may be common
to you, and totems to me,
hoarding treasure in a tree
like I bureau a poem.
I don't expect a murder of crows
from the lost ebony feathers.
I covet it like treasure, even though
Poe heard omens calling ravens,
even though I just channeled
their mourning clothes
while on the phone.

However, the crow reminds me
to be mindful of the present,
even as I ask what harm
exists in looking back,
as caws crack sidewalks
and rake sky, and squirrels
buzz and squawk in shifting Pines,

as sap-soaked cones drop
like silent bombs on lawns,
even as I circle back to crows
and poems and phone calls,
to soles painted caution yellow
in classic human distraction.

Spell

The familiar beach house,
scent wave of vanilla sunscreen,
eggs, toast, potatoes, and coffee.
I smell with every pore in my body,
sails me to the kitchen table
for a family card game.

While I am adrift at the table,
the card game enchants,
suits skip like waves running
underneath reversing breaks.
The spell is impossible to hold,
the magic wears off,
an uneven hand wins
the game, ninety-nine.

We laugh until we cry
with pleasure so keen,
it wakes me
from a dream.

After Reading a Bazooka Bubble Gum Wrapper

Peeling off the pink wrapper,
Your future lies before you,
takes me back to high school,
when college hovered
like senior year head shots
in the proofs from which I chose
the sense of self I hoped to grow into.

Shading SAT's gray spaces
taught me left-brain logic
that a four-year university
would corroborate,
while my right brain's
imminent creativity
strained at the leash,
like a helium balloon
eager to fly.

Which headshot,
which perfect smile,
which college,
will fly me to the future,
where I realize
the freedom to write
and revise my life
as I would have it.

Body Politic

Post-Roe, when Ruth Bader Ginsberg argued
voting rights to *Time Magazine:* "the law
a vehicle for moving the country forward,"
I felt my sole pressing an imaginary gas pedal,
Ruth's words riding next to me, my hair streaming
in the cool air of our new freedoms.

Post-Dobbs, Ruth gone,
the soft animal of my body feels invaded
by the powers that be of the Supreme Court,
robed grim reapers standing
between me and invading weeds
penetrating sidewalk cracks,
naked to injudicious invasions
they may care to make into me.

Post-Dobbs, Ruth gone,
I pause at an octagonal sign
saying STOP—as the belly
of a carbon monoxide breeze
swells against me, filling my vehicle
with deadly intent, forcing me
to abandon what I thought was safety
to flee—I hope not into the arms
of my would-be captors.

A Call of the Wild

Stillness sits like a Buddha
on the moon's other side.

I can't hear the barn owl flying over me,
but it probably hears my breathing,
like a hurricane among the pines.

Somewhere there must be a world
untouched by human hands,

nature free to evolve
without damage,

On the moon's other side is where I'll be,
barely touching lunar soil with my feet,
collecting bright unkempt moonlight
for all that's dark on the horizon.

Country Road

The road's curve compels me to bend,
slowing to twenty-five from fifty-five,
smelling the sun-saturated tar,
hearing the purring trees,
as daisies and dandelions nod
across the pollened air at us,
bending to the breeze.

Around a corner, houses
and traffic peter out and fields reign,
vined weeds wind
wild shrubs and trees.

Let me learn to live
in the curves, one with the landscape
before—and someday after—
prime real estate made
to accommodate condominiums or cell towers
returns to nature. Let me be
at home where wild daisies
smell of yesterday.

Now and Again

The dogwood tree's blush colors
pressed like a memory,
pressed like a memory on Mom's face,
gathered at the edges of her eyes and lips.
The curves of her mouth
imprinted in rose pink,
light maroon, on drinking glasses.
Cherry blossom colors mine,
plump lips reflecting her long ago,
like beauty's timekeeper.

Between this Year and Next

In the fog I navigate
between this new year
and the next,
last year's resolutions star
and crust my windshield
like un-swept bugs.

I guess the universe makes
no distinctions between the loss
of a resolution, insect or star—
each sloughing
and regrowth of skin cells
on its vast expanding body.

The billions of years it takes
for a star to form from nebulae,
to burn till it cools
and dwindles or explodes
and grow new stars
as identical to itself
as one bug on my window,

and one human pausing
to glance at its might,
covering one eye with a hand
that occludes and reveals,
one eye that can choose one star
from the multitude to imagine.

To Make Sacred

Sometimes, to be apart
from tradition,
a universe sometimes foreign
shares a story,
where borders and belonging dissolve,
and remembers communion
in a wedding service.

I'm remembering communion
in a Catholic church
on Ann Street before
I questioned belief.
The priest prepares
for the marriage sacrament,
blesses us
for not being Catholic.

Long ago, blessed nonetheless,
when rolling under pews
beyond my parents' reach,
wafers and wine
tasted of dust and vinegar
I grimaced in tonguing.

That dissonance as a child,
the lack of faith,
the pretense, the lapsing,
all sacred as naves,
as every bone in the body,
as the news of everything
true and everything askew
in the world, a wasteland
of news waiting
for something to grace it
with scattered petals
on the church aisle.

Cicada

Its leftover molt
presses the garage door
as if to seek entry.
Outside the window
its fresh exoskeleton
clicks music
even the fan can't
distract us from.
Our house feels as hollow
as that molt
the day we move out.
The cicadas shrill
from among the violet clematis
threading the lattice,
as if to urge us out,
as dusk winds the day down,
as we shake off
the old shell
and try our wings.

Summer Prayer

Let the geranium petals
hueing the porch
keep flaming apricot
in their basket.

Nothing in this moment
of heat, light and shadow
is yet past, though soon
new moments
will abandon them
to memory.

Keep the flowers
from wilting,
as I fold my hands
under their basket's shadow
in the heat that wants
its way with them.

The heat that wants
its way with them
has its way with us,
slicked with a membrane
of sweat's stickiness.
Sounds spill from streets,
giving us reasons to praise
their music: sirens
en route to fires,
hydrants extolling water
fountain hot bodies.

Car horns vibrate
between houses,
as somewhere
in these moments
of heat and music
I find myself in prayer.

The Snail

A snail crossing a sidewalk
caught me with slimy trails
glimmering in the early sun,

a sacred message
of passage
as the snail glides on concrete.

Tentacles scent
green frequencies
of grass blades,
see possibility in a leaf,
sketching luster
on the bumpy pavement.

Movement on Squares in Dupont Circle

Another universe plays out
under shady trees
nature never intended.

Wind tosses
a cacophony of leaves,
small talk imbues
a pawn's move
or queen's travel
over checkered tables
with bettors' adrenalin.

Then stumbles,
square upon square
on ancient history lessons,
like Queen Elizabeth into monarchy.
There is more
than a chessboard
of square victories
and defeats in each of us.

In a universe of pawning
for a rook or knight,
how easily
a chess game shows me
what I should divest,
and let the what remain mysterious.

Crossing the Lines

When I reread
a 1991 article on violence,
it hasn't aged
one bit, a gun
stealing lives.
Yellow tape communicates
where the deceased lie.
Why does the tale revive itself?
But not why—
why are we idle?

I've never owned a gun,
but does that absolve me?
Who will revive
the human race,
and who watches
their backs to stay alive?
When turning to police
for justice, who will feel
a foreigner in their own land?
Is dissonant behavior the shape
of a gun's intent,
rather than an embrace of belonging?

When I read a six-year-old
shot his teacher,
I dreamed of Valentines or apples,
any random act of kindness
that crosses the lines
of separation.

New Clothes, Old Letters

The smell of new shoes, a sleeveless dress,
the manufacturer's fragrance
cloaking the closet's usual scent.
Embroidered fabric
with tangled waist strings,
intoxicating leather fumes
woo feet to slide in,
make them feel needed.

The dress oozes from the hanger
like a chanteuse mouthing a vowel.
Behind the old shoebox of letters
is the new box of shoes.

Is the box of handwritten letters
fashioned, self-expression or acting,
or an exercise in self-seduction,
love notes proving true as the new you,
stepping into new shoes,
re-entering the world like a page awaiting a pen.

Threshold

Recently the waves crested at four feet,
froth chewing sand like a rabid bubble bath,
leaving a wrack line of augur, clam, scallop,
and sand dollar shells the tide's retreat reveals.

Swells' blue deepens to a hue
that won't stay for even a day, changing
with every variation of light and darkness.

Swimming under water bejeweled
by jellyfish masquerading as breath,
I move to the breaking waves' rhythm,
as if I live there, but knowing it isn't home.

Sea crosses shore's threshold
between the known and mystery,
and the edge where each begins and ends
in waves molding granules of sand—
formless, formed, erosive,
possessed, unpossessed.

Ferris Wheel

The carnival harbors
on the boardwalk
at dawn, warm breezes
peel away the cold months,

undressing anticipation
of layered clothing,
doughy donuts frying,
sticky cotton candy clouds
awaiting eager lips.
Hints of stale cigarette smoke,
linger in a breeze.

The Ferris wheel looks skeletal
without its seats—hibernating
who knows where—while I sit
on concrete, a breeze pushing my hair
around my face as I imagine my next ride
high over the boardwalk,
when truffles of happy tourists
will sweeten sidewalks.

The missing seats woo me
with their in-between,
the possibilities of the bardo
before the carnival opens.

Us

Wax widens
the solitary candle's circle,

drips around its base
as the flame illuminates your face.

I trust you to every o'clock,
as the small hand stops telling time.

Outside, bare paper waits.
As I photograph
the paper birch,

I see what anchors us
in the way its bark sloughs
as the tree expands.

I wonder how it knows
the right moment to expose its new skin

to the forest,
to the us of trees.

Freedom Meditation

In the land
of many flags,
sweet tea, ice cream,
and sculpted bushes,
can you feel your freedoms?

I feel violins' vibration
awaken
what's nestled along
the Cape Fear River.
Boats' bones crack
across the riverbank.
American flag
flies on the pole,
unforsaken in air.
Freedom asks me
to jump
into the river
with abandon.

Freedom asks me
to step off the beaten path
to mediate meaning away,

to feel pebbles
wash my hands raw,
warbling through fingers.
Freedom awakens the sleepy
sitting by the river
like a melody.
Open your eyes
and sing what you see.

A Prayer

Solicit moon's solitude as a prayer for the body,
see the moon in its white light, the woods turning gray,
something that sways the mind's curtains,
soul blowing through an open window.

See in this moonlit night a living archetype
shaping new lands from dark's molten flow.

Though the moonlight casts the shadows
of condominiums and stores,
they feel manmade, alien as another planet's shadow.

Stand still wherever you are and listen
to your heart beating in the seashells of your ears.
Wake up and listen as the ocean tides' kaleidoscope
crescendoes among generations of beach grass.

Cherry Blossoms

Your blooms unravel
at spring's cusp,
making trees blush,
unraveling something
pulled too tight in me.

I uncoil so far
that I run along
green Washington lawns
under your pink umbrellas.

Cast your beauty
at my feet, like raindrops
of tiny scented handkerchiefs.
Mesmerize the eye
of sunlit sky, open
to your frolics.

I am lost in your resurgence
and don't want to be found.
Cover me with your supple petals,
faint me with your fragrance.

Alive me.
Unravel me to life.

Knowing what awaits,
not even one petal
fears
death's unraveling.
Consecrate me

with the water and the sun,
the earthworms and pollinators,
seduce me, as time
stitches winter's seams
into spring's pleats,
dressing trees
in pink ballgowns,
lining the lawns
I dance on.

About the Author

Holli Terrell-Cavalluzzi lives in Wilmington, North Carolina. She is pursuing her MFA in creative writing.

Her poems have appeared in *Flora Fiction, New Note Poetry,* and *Quillkeepers Press: Myth and Lore Anthology.* Her book of poetry, *Lotus Bloom,* was independently published in 2021.

www.ingramcontent.com/pod-product-compliance
Lightning Source LLC
Chambersburg PA
CBHW030814090426
42737CB00010B/1273